Newbury in the 1950s

Tony Higgott

COUNTRYSIDE BOOKS
NEWBURY BERKSHIRE

First published 2004
© Tony Higgott, 2004

COUNTRYSIDE BOOKS
3 Catherine Road
Newbury, Berkshire

To view our complete range of books,
please visit us at
www.countrysidebooks.co.uk

ISBN 1 85306 887 X

The cover picture shows Cheap Street in 1955
(courtesy of Jim Irving)

Produced through MRM Associates Ltd., Reading
Printed by J. W. Arrowsmith, Bristol

NEWBURY IN THE 1950s

The 1950s was a decade when fundamental changes occurred which were to shape modern Newbury. Like the rest of the country, the town was recovering from the effects of the Second World War. It had not suffered unduly from enemy bombing, but large areas of its countryside were still occupied by army and air force bases. Clothing, food and raw materials, such as steel and timber, for the manufacturing, building and printing industries were in short supply and for individuals and companies alike, the supply of these essential commodities was controlled by rationing.

The *Newbury Weekly News* in 1950 carried a 'Lost & Found' column for objects such as a lady's brown glove or a pair of baby's blue shoes. This showed the seriousness of such loss, not solely on account of cost, but because of the difficulty of sparing clothing coupons to purchase replacements. It also shows that it was anticipated that someone would have picked up and handed in, or safely kept, the lost item. Each week there were several advertisements for second-hand clothes for sale which, of course, did not require coupons. In October 1950 the *NWN* was forced, by the rationing of newsprint, to either cut the size of the paper from eight pages to six, or reduce its print run. It chose the latter and advised its readers to place orders with their newsagent as there would be few spare copies.

In the same month the Government announced that there was insufficient electricity generating capacity and in fairness to all consumers a rota of what was euphemistically called 'load-shedding' was announced. This meant that everyone would suffer one day (and possibly two) when there was likely to be no electricity supplied between 7.30 am and 9 am, at lunchtime, and again from 6.30 pm until 9 pm. Most of Newbury would be without supplies on Tuesdays (and Fridays, if necessary); and the Andover Road, Valley Road and Wash Common areas on Thursdays (and possibly Tuesdays). It was in this era that the Government embarked on the building of giant power stations to replace the many small local ones. The new ones were mainly in the Midlands and north (Didcot was later) and were coal-fired. Also in October 1950, it was stated that Harwell AERE was considering if the heat from atomic piles could be used to generate electricity. It was in 1956 when the world's first nuclear power station, Calder Hall in Cumbria, began to operate, so government, scientific and political 'consideration' must have started well before 1950. The initial reason for needing the Calder Hall reactor was to produce plutonium for atomic weapons which was, no doubt, the spur to its construction.

Of more lasting concern was the shortage of housing. Six years of war during which many romances had been 'on hold' led to a spate of marriages in the mid/late 1940s, quickly followed by the starting of new families – otherwise known as the 'Baby Boom'. Some families, desperate for space, squatted in the barrack huts of abandoned military bases such as RAF Greenham. Many young couples shared the homes of one of their parents. In other instances local authorities erected surplus army huts to provide housing. These were seen as a stop-gap and throughout the 1950s councils tried to obtain Government sanction to build permanent dwellings to rehouse these families. Each year the Government would agree to a specific number of houses being built – a small number of private dwellings, but the majority council housing. The latter were then allocated to people with the greatest need. In January 1950 it was reported that 138 houses had been built on the Shaw estate. A month later the Ministry of Health authorised the building of 66 three-bedroom houses, 10 old people's dwellings and a block of six lock-up shops with flats over at Shaw, and eight private houses within the borough. In January, it was also reported that the council discussed whether the County Council should be asked if they wished to acquire a site for a community centre on the Shaw estate and if a site should be offered to brewery companies for building a public house. The latter was ruled out as a councillor said that there were many pubs within a reasonable distance of the estate, including four in Shaw Crescent and that housing should be given absolute priority. In October 1950, Newbury Borough had a waiting list of 1,015 people

and the adjacent Rural Councils a further 1,854. One can understand councillors feeling that they should concentrate on the 'pressing demand for living accommodation' but throughout the country local authorities were criticised for building housing estates, with facilities, including shops, as an afterthought.

Despite the apparent problems of the era, people were still able to enjoy a wide variety of entertainment. Films were a great draw and Newbury had three cinemas, until fire destroyed the Carlton in Cheap Street, in May 1950. Professional and amateur musical and dramatic events were staged at the Corn Exchange and the Plaza Theatre (almost next to the Corn Exchange). Regular visitors to the latter were Salisbury Arts Theatre Company. Newbury String Players, a professional group of musicians formed by the composer Gerald Finzi gave performances in the town and the long-established amateur group, Newbury Symphony Orchestra, also employed professional conductors and soloists. However, most entertainment was provided by amateur groups and several local firms had their own dramatic societies. Remembered with great fondness by audiences and participants are the pantomimes staged by France Belk. The Corn Exchange was also a venue for dances, balls and dinners. In 1950 the council spent around £6,000 on renovations, including a false ceiling and internal redecoration to provide modern facilities.

The recreation ground at Wash Common was formed

in 1950 from 'scrub and gorse into an excellent playing field with facilities for football'. A considerable contribution to the cost was raised voluntarily by the inhabitants of Wash Common. In February 1950 the Borough Council was looking forward to Greenham Common being returned to them. It was reported that gun platforms, air raid shelters and building foundations had been removed and they were eager to restore it once again to 'a thing of beauty'. Then, in March 1951, the Government announced that a new airfield was to be built on Greenham and Crookham commons. An immediate allocation of 42 houses was made to Newbury Rural District Council, to rehouse the people living in huts who would be made homeless. Although Newbury Borough owned the common, it lay within the administrative area of Newbury RDC.

The new airfield, with its 2½ mile long runway, was required because of the 'Cold War' between the West and the Soviet Bloc. USAF B47 bombers and their supporting KC97 fuel tanker aircraft used the airfield, though formally it was an RAF station. An accident occurred in 1958 when a B47 jettisoned two fuel tanks. The fire that resulted burned for 16 hours and destroyed two other B47s on the ground, one of which was carrying a nuclear weapon. At the time it was not acknowledged that there were nuclear weapons at Greenham.

The Festival of Britain, in 1951, was promoted by the Government as a celebration of the British way of life, to raise spirits after the war and act as a showcase for British capabilities in the fields of manufacturing and modern design. In this it echoed the Great Exhibition of a century earlier. It was centred on the South Bank in London, where the Royal Festival Hall is a tangible remain. An aim of the Festival was that each community would play an individual part. Initially the Borough Council appeared unenthusiastic but following a meeting of local societies and organisations, chaired by the Mayor (Jack Hole), the Borough took the lead in planning Newbury's celebrations. These were held from 10th to 24th June and the fortnight was packed with events. Highlights were the opening ball, which included the crowning of the Festival Queen (Pauline Port) at the Corn Exchange, with around 800 people gathered to see her and her attendants cross the Market Place; 2,500 people saw grass-track motor cycle racing; 1,000 churchgoers formed a Procession of Witness through the town and were joined by another 4,000 in Victoria Park to hear short addresses from Anglican and Free Church speakers; 8,560 visited an exhibition of Arts, Crafts, Hobbies, etc, at the Corn Exchange; and the largest provincial Veteran Car Rally was held, comprising 68 cars, the oldest being an 8HP 2 cylinder Lux of 1895. The rally ended with a parade which passed between large crowds lining Northbrook Street. On the final day there was a Carnival Procession with nearly 50 lorry or trailer-borne tableaux, decorated cars and cycles, four marching bands, six jazz bands and two 'old time' orchestras. It was led by the Craven

Hounds and 40 or 50 mounted huntsmen. The procession was one and a half miles long and took 50 minutes to pass. A crowd, estimated at 35,000, watched the procession and afterwards thronged the Market Place for singing, dancing and fireworks. Late buses were laid on and coaches brought people from as far afield as Reading and Whitchurch. Two years later, in June 1953, a parade of 60 decorated vehicles was held as part of the celebrations to mark the Coronation of Queen Elizabeth II. The day was scheduled to end with a fireworks display at Newbury Town Football Club. In view of the wet weather this was postponed to the following day, unfortunately no one told the public – or the police – and hundreds of people turned up and waited and waited! Many street parties were held and Newbury's biggest party, for 600 old people, included lunch at the Corn Exchange. The Coronation was the first big televised event. Many of the fortunate few to own a set invited friends and neighbours to watch the Coronation service and the royal procession to and from Westminster Abbey. The event proved a boost to television ownership.

An unexpected announcement was made in the House of Commons in April 1950, when it was stated that an Atomic Energy Research Establishment was to be created on the former war-time airfield at Aldermaston (work had begun at Harwell AERE in 1946). No mention was made at this stage that the Aldermaston facility was to specialise in atomic weapons research.

Concerns expressed locally were about the loss of facilities and the effect on the availability of labour during its building. Bradfield RDC sent a resolution to the Prime Minister and the local MP requesting that labour be employed 'from as far away as possible from this area', so that men from local building trades or agricultural work would not be attracted by the higher wages offered. In response, the Berkshire secretary of the National Union of Agricultural Workers suggested that the RDC's concerns could be met by employers increasing agricultural wages. Newbury was directly affected when, in July, the Ministry of Supply announced they were to build 200 houses for staff of the new establishment. In January 1951 the *Newbury Weekly News* reported that the Ministry had submitted plans of the new housing for the authority's information – they had no power to refuse or modify them. One hundred and four semi-detached houses were to be built for senior staff off Wendan Road and 120 permanent pre-fabricated houses in blocks of four as an extension to Valley Road, linking it to Essex Street. Fortunately, the council welcomed the development as an asset to the town, it was felt that the occupants would benefit trade and the new estates would enable those parts of the town to be developed.

Educational establishments were also being improved. In 1950 the building of Winchcombe Primary School, to serve the Shaw Estate, was under way and in October of that year it was agreed that the building at Park House of a new secondary school for boys would start the following year. This would enable Shaw House School to become girls only. Shaw House had been commandeered in 1943 as a replacement for the bombed Council Secondary Schools. Plans were published in May 1951 for the substantial extension of South Berkshire College, to cater for the growing demand for further education. In particular skilled scientific and electrical workers were in short supply locally and so, of high priority, was to be the building of laboratory and workshop blocks. These would total 14,000 square feet and cost £80,000 – 60% of which would be paid by the Ministry of Education, the balance from Berkshire County funds. Eventually other new buildings, costing an estimated £150,000, would provide facilities for a wide range of subjects. In July 1950 HRH Princess Margaret opened the Mary Hare Grammar School for deaf pupils, which had moved into Arlington Manor the previous September.

The 1950s was also an era when improvement and modernisation of towns themselves were planned. In the case of Newbury this included removal of through traffic from the three main shopping streets. These streets were then also residential streets as there were many rows of cottages behind the shops. An outline plan for the development of Newbury into a town of 24,000 inhabitants had been agreed in 1949. The population of the Borough was 17,772 in the 1951 census and had grown to 20,397 by 1961, but not until the early 1970s

did it reach 24,000. Continuing with the plan to develop the town, in July 1950, the council considered a zoning plan drawn up by the County Planning Officer. This was for the area encompassed by the proposed northern and eastern relief roads, the railway line and Northcroft Park. Although the shopping area was to be increased, looking back from the 21st century it is surprising to see that it was then proposed to continue the intermixing of industry and commerce in the central area. The substantial woodworking firm, Elliotts of Newbury, was to the west of Northbrook Street and an industrial area based on their site was to be extended south to Northcroft Lane. The land south of the lane was to become open space. A new cattle market was to be built east of the relief road and the area of the former site, in Market Street, extended southwards to the railway station, zoned for light industry (later changed to 'general business'). The area that is now occupied by Camp Hopson's furniture department and car park was proposed for new civic offices, whilst the whole of Newbury Wharf was earmarked for public building, including a car park and a new bus station. Two other sites for public building were located near the new relief roads. The fire station moved from The Wharf to its new site in the late 1950s, but the police station was not opened in Mill Lane until 1965. A large maltings, Whitehorn's bakery and a milk-bottling and distribution depot remained to the west of Bartholomew Street and a large area centred on these was scheduled

7

for warehouses. The heavy engineering works of Plenty & Co was then still located between Bartholomew Street and Cheap Street, but moved out to Hambridge Road in 1965. The idea of planning the town's development did not meet with total approval, as an irate letter in the *NWN* of 13th July 1950 shows: 'How dare we think of town planning while our people live in Nissen huts and our cemetery is a hayfield?'

New roads to take traffic from the town were included in the plan, but it was the late 1950s before the northern relief road opened as Western Avenue and 1966 when the first section of the eastern relief road was completed.

The volume of road traffic today makes it hard to envisage that the A34 passed through the centre of the town, from Newtown Road to Oxford Road. The route of the A4 was from London Road via Broadway and Old Bath Road to its present line. The A339 commenced at the Town Hall and then via Cheap Street and Greenham Road, crossed Greenham Common and went on to Basingstoke. Re-routing of this was brought about in the early 1950s by the enlargement of Greenham Common airfield. A new road was built from the Swan pub at Newtown and the road across the Common closed. In an attempt to reduce congestion, in March 1950 a one-way system was introduced, northwards in Bartholomew Street and southwards in Cheap Street and east along Market Street. Newbury's first traffic lights were switched on in 1957, to control traffic at the junction of Market Street and Bartholomew Street. From 1945 to 1950, south-bound traffic was diverted from Oxford Road via Love Lane, Turnpike Road, Fir Tree Lane, Hambridge Road and Stroud Green from Easter to the end of September. It was discontinued as the police found difficulty in enforcing it. Traffic today is much heavier than in the 1950s, but even then road accidents were frequent and deaths reported in almost every edition of the local newspaper.

Newbury's bus station was then at The Wharf, with offices in the Granary building. There were regular services throughout the town and to west Berkshire and Hampshire villages as, in the early 1950s, few people owned cars, though many used cycles for personal transport. In the 1950s Newbury train station served a railway junction. In addition to the Western Region main line from London to the south-west peninsula, the line from Didcot to Winchester, linking the industrial Midlands to the port of Southampton, passed through the town. There was also the branch line to Lambourn, serving people living in the villages of the Lambourn Valley, as well as the racehorse training industry, whose animals were transported by rail to race meetings throughout the country. In the late 1940s commercial use of the Kennet and Avon Canal had been revived. John Gould was operating a pair of boats from Newbury and beginning to acquire a regular trade. Another carrier, John Knill, had brought 20 tons of salt from Cheshire for Newbury Laundry in February 1950, intending that this should become a regular contract.

This infant trading was dealt a body blow by the announcement that the waterway would be closed from 14th July 1950, due to the unsafe condition of Burghfield and Heale's locks and the need to replace the gates of other locks. The subsequent story of the battle to keep the canal open and then restore it is too long to be told here but, as is well known, ends successfully with the restored canal being opened in 1990.

In the 21st century we take for granted that branches of the same shops and stores will be found in most town centres and out of town developments. Half a century ago the majority of Newbury shops was owned by local people. True, there were branches of Boots, Marks and Spencer, WH Smith, Woolworth and several grocery chains (mostly swallowed by the supermarket giants of later years) and others such as Macfisheries and Timothy Whites (chemists) which no longer exist, but individual businesses predominated. Camp Hopson's department store continues to be successful in local ownership, but Davies's china shop, Dexter Robinson's (outfitters and haberdashers), the House of Toomer (ironmongers, hardware, paint, electrical and garden machinery) and the Tudor Café – which played such a big part in the cultural life of the town – have all gone from Northbrook Street. Beynon's (outfitters), Hickman & Metcalf (ironmongers etc) and even larger businesses not Newbury-owned, like WJ Daniel (clothing and furniture) and Reading Co-op, have gone from Market Place. Throughout the town numerous butchers, greengrocers, newsagent and tobacconists, sweet shops, shoe repairers and other small businesses have all closed down, some through the competitive pricing of supermarkets, others because of changes in society – how many people today have their shoes re-soled, rather than buy new ones?

Some indication of the costs of goods and housing and of wages paid can be gleaned from reports and advertisements in the *Newbury Weekly News*. From April 1951, the Town Clerk and the Borough Treasurer of Newbury were each paid £1,151 p.a., though the Clerk's salary scale continued by £50 per annum increments to £1,300. March 1950 saw the Head Cook's post at Kingsclere hospital (catering for staff and a maximum of 100 patients) advertised at £6.12s 0d per week (£343 p.a.) – females would be paid £65 p.a. less! A Hercules bicycle cost £11 and a 16 inch Qualcast motor mower £45, whilst a simple hand lawnmower was £3. All could be bought from Currys. A Bush TV, with 7¼ inch x 6 inch screen cost 49 guineas and Heather's advertised smart tweed coats, the new shorter length, for £4.11s.6d and flowered silk frocks for £2.10s.0d. In March 1950, a four bedroom detached house with bathroom and large garden, between Newbury and Thatcham was for sale at £3,250. At the same time A W Neate and Sons were advertising a 'beautiful stone-built Queen Anne house in Wiltshire', with nine bedrooms, two bathrooms etc, garages and stabling, an entrance lodge and cottage, together with

six acres of grounds and paddocks at £12,500. Large houses were seen as an expensive liability at the time. The Borough was able to build 58 houses in Love Lane, in 1951, at a cost of about £2,770 for a pair of semi-detached and £4,548 for a block of four.

At the beginning of the 21st century concern is expressed about the lack of public involvement with political matters. It is therefore surprising to learn that prior to the General Election of February 1950, around 700 people (including 150 standing) attended a discussion held at the Corn Exchange between the Liberal and Labour candidates; the Conservative candidate declined to take part. Both candidates were supported by two 'men from Oxford'. Those supporting the Liberal being Mr Jeremy Thorpe and Mr Robin Day! Both later achieved fame, Thorpe as leader of the Liberal party and Day as a leading political commentator and TV personality. At the election itself there was a turnout of 81% of the electorate. The seat was won by the Conservative, Mr Anthony Hurd (later Lord Hurd) with 18,150 votes; the Liberal had 11,914 and Labour 4,284 votes.

Newbury faced the challenges of the 1950s with optimism and enthusiasm and the photographs on the following pages give a glimpse into that life. I hope you enjoy them. They have been gathered from a number of sources and on page 94 I have pleasure in acknowledging the kind assistance of all those who have made the book possible.

Tony Higgott

Newbury from the west with West Mills and the swing bridge in the foregound and Town Mills and St Nicolas church beyond. From 1921 to 1957 both mills were operated by Hovis; Town Mills producing bread flour and West Mills animal feed. The long-established local firm H Dolton & Son Ltd purchased both mills when Hovis left. Mr Williams, the photographer, frequently had his carefully composed views reproduced in the *Newbury Weekly News*. *Photograph by Stanley Williams. West Berkshire Museum. L 127*

Whilst this photograph of Town Mill was taken earlier than the 1950s, it shows the mill complex as it appeared in that decade. The large building on the left, where the milling took place, was constructed in 1892 following a major fire. For centuries the river had turned a water-wheel to power the millstones which ground wheat into flour. By the 1950s the river's flow was used to drive a powerful turbine linked to a generator. This produced 45 kilowatts of electricity and supplied the milling machines that produced the flour, as well as other equipment. The building with the 'Hovis' sign was the 18th century miller's house. To its right another 18th century building had been converted to garages. *West Berkshire Museum 1983.29.2*

During the Second World War, the Rivers Kennet and Thames formed a barrier across southern England, which was made defendable in case of invasion. Numerous concrete 'Pillbox' gun emplacements were built, one can be seen in the centre of this photograph. The heavy concrete blocks were ready in strategic positions to form 'tank traps'. These were on the north side of the river, to the east of Victoria Park. In the background are Holland's Mill and Greenham Mills. *Jim Irving 119*

John Gould's boats *Colin* and *Iris* passing Victoria park. The wartime anti-tank defences can clearly be seen.
West Berkshire Museum 1993.37.1

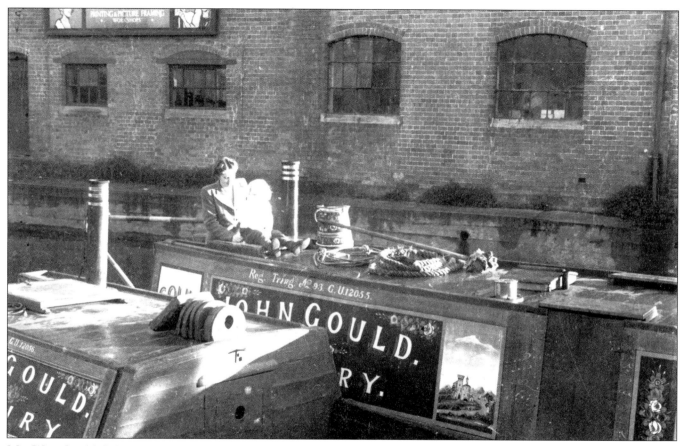

Mrs Wyn Gould, John's wife, with one of her children on their boat *Colin*, in 1949, *Iris* is in the foreground. W H Smith's printing works (adjacent to Lloyds Bank) is in the background. *West Berkshire Museum, J Gould Collection 1992.34.2*

John Gould started a business hiring rowing boats after the closure of the Kennet & Avon Canal prevented him from pursuing his canal carrying business. This photograph, taken about 1952, shows John standing against his floating office. Although the boats were moored in mid-stream at night, they were often found lodged against down-stream weirs after they had been let loose. *West Berkshire Museum, J Gould Collection 1992.34.*

Northbrook Street in 1954. The excellent Tudor Café, which also provided a meeting place in the town, is to the left. Jack Hole, its joint proprietor, was an active borough councillor and is the only surviving individual to be honoured with the Freedom of the Borough of Newbury. *Jim Irving 3*□

East side of Northbrook Street in 1959. Camp Hopson's department store remains, but the other shops have all undergone change. Liddiard's butchers shop on Newbury Bridge is now Costa Coffee, the House of Toomer after contracting in scope and moving to Bartholomew Street is no more (except that its name is preserved by Barry Forkin's locksmith's business). Boots and Timothy Whites, who ran very similar businesses, merged and their premises were rebuilt in the 1970s.

Jim Irving 291□

18

Toomer's the long-established and much used ironmongers, hardware, heating, paint and electrical store in Northbrook Street, was severely damaged by fire on 20th April 1961 and subsequently rebuilt. *West Berkshire Museum 2001.42.2*

The combined bands of the Scots Guards and Irish Guards marching down Northbrook Street in September 1957, before appearing at the Newbury Agricultural Show, held at Elcot Park. To the right, a van is emerging from Jack Street, one of the streets of cottages in the town which have long been demolished. *A Freeman Ltd photograph.*
West Berkshire Museum 1979.72.170

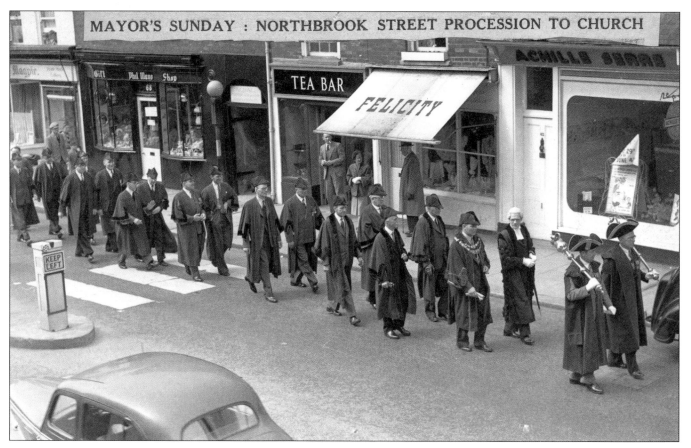

MAYOR'S SUNDAY : NORTHBROOK STREET PROCESSION TO CHURCH

Newbury borough councillors and aldermen being led along Northbrook Street in 1954 by the mace-bearers and the mayor (Cllr Huckle) on their way to the Mayor's Sunday service at the Methodist Church. *F C Strutt photograph. West Berkshire Museum 1979.72.146*

21

Northbrook Street, west side, north of West Street. Few photographs appear to have survived of this part of the street and the buildings behind the hoardings were demolished in 1966. The stone-faced building (dated 1834) housed the Newbury Literary and Scientific Institute from its foundation in 1843. Next to it is the former Liberal Club. Extreme left is Davies and Son's china shop (with a grapevine growing inside), which was demolished about 1990 and a McDonald's branch was built on its site. *West Berkshire Museum 2004.50.298*

The Clocktower at the Broadway. Martin & Chillingworth's garage is to the left and Wheeler's garage is behind the photographer. Repairs formed a major part of a garage's business in the 1950s (and later) and they were therefore usually established on main roads. *Jim Irving photograph. West Berkshire Museum 1986.56.8*

Northbrook Street from the Broadway. This photograph was possibly taken in the 1940s, but typifies the busy junction of the A4 and A34 in the holiday season. Leather cases stacked on the luggage rack of the car in the centre and luggage projecting from the boot of the one to the left, reminds us of the improvements made to the carrying capacity of cars.

West Berkshire Museum 2000.20.7

Northbrook Street, probably the same day as the photograph opposite and possibly a Saturday as there are few commercial vehicles. A traffic census, carried out over two twelve-hour periods on a Friday and Saturday in 1954, found that almost 26,500 cars and motorcycles, 1,734 buses and coaches, 6,000 goods vehicles and nearly 7,000 cycles, an actual total of 41,444 vehicles, passed the Clocktower. *West Berkshire Museum 2000.20.8*

Apart from the volume of through traffic, Newbury's 18th century bridge over the River Kennet had to carry heavy loads. This pull-push transport, heading north in 1956, also had to take care not to 'ground' on the apex of the bridge. *Jim Irving 15*

This very long construction, possibly heading for the Esso refinery at Fawley, near Southampton in 1960, would have caused long delays whilst it manoeuvred around the corner into Mansion House Street. It is believed that the police would have directed loads such as this against the usual one-way traffic flow in Bartholomew Street. *Jim Irving 77*

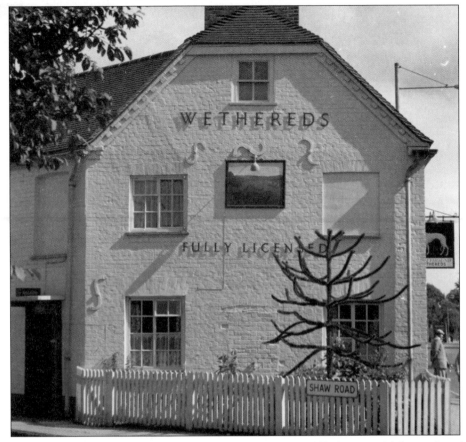

This 1957 photograph shows the Shaw Road elevation of The Greyhound public house, which stood at the junction with London Road. With adjacent property (see next pages) it was demolished for the building of a roundabout at the junction of the two relief roads. *West Berkshire Museum 1979.72.326*

The Greyhound and Miss Elsie Harrison's Handy Stores in London Road in 1957. Both were demolished in the early 1960s for the construction of the Robin Hood roundabout. *Jim Irving 143*□

The Robin Hood pub which gave its name to the roundabout, taken 1957. The building was demolished, along with those shown in the photograph on page 29 and several cottages at the end of Shaw Crescent. The licence was transferred to a nearby private house, The Myrtles, which became the present Robin Hood/Harvester. *Jim Irving 143*□

The Old Armoury, Kings Road. This building, erected around 1800, was once used by the Newbury Company of the 4th Royal Berkshire Regiment. It appears to have been originally part of the maltsters premises owned by Baird & Sons in the 1950s. Malting was once an important trade in Newbury, its product being sold to London brewers as well as more locally. The building was demolished to make way for the relief road and stood where Sainsbury's car park is now. *Jim Irving 32*

Serious flooding occurred more frequently than now. This shows Bartholomew Street, just south of the railway bridge, probably in 1955. *West Berkshire Museum 1989.60.2*

Flooding to gardens of houses in Russell Road, 1955. The photograph also shows that many people grew their own vegetables, particularly Brussels sprouts and other members of the cabbage family. *Jim Irving 40*□

Flooding at Elliotts of Newbury factory (late 1950s or early 60s), showing damage to sophisticated wood-working machinery and stocks of part-made furniture. Elliotts were high quality furniture manufacturers, and Newbury's largest employer in the 1950s and 1960s. During the 1939–45 war they had transferred production to making troop-carrying gliders and aircraft. When timber supplies for furniture were limited by government controls in the late 1940s, they turned to making sports and training gliders (see photo opposite), which continued alongside furniture manufacture until the mid-1960s. *Elliotts of Newbury archive. West Berkshire Museum*

The Olympia 'EoN', holder of ten British gliding records.

An Olympia 'EoN' sailplane (or glider), made by Elliotts of Newbury and one of only four aircraft shown in the Transport Pavilion at the 1951 Festival of Britain exhibition in London. The famous Schneider Trophy winner of the 1930s can be glimpsed at the right. The Olympia gliders were successfully used in many international competitions and the RAF purchased a large number of training gliders. *Elliotts of Newbury archive. West Berkshire Museum*

Many in Newbury were employed in several large engineering companies. Newbury Diesel Company was in King's Road (where the entrance to Sainsbury's premises and their petrol station are now). Founded in 1932, they made engines ranging from small portable units for farms and commercial use to engines for coastal shipping, which were up to 1680 HP. The photograph shows the main bay of the factory with an 'O' type engine being rebuilt in the right foreground and a 'P' type beyond. *West Berkshire Museum 1989.11.23*

A large 'P' type ship's engine on a test bed, 1955. Note its size from the previous photograph, which shows a man standing beside a similar engine. In 1964 the company first manufactured ships' remote control gear (operated from the bridge) and in 1967 ceased to make engines, as they felt no longer able to compete with the large manufacturers.
West Berkshire Museum 1989.11.126

Newbury Market Place in 1956. Fisher's caravan in the centre is a butcher's stall, whilst C A Austin's van states 'cut price grocer & provision merchant' and 'Bacon a speciality'. Other stalls sell fruit and vegetables, fabric, clothing and flowers, much as today. To the right can be seen the entrance passageway to the Plaza theatre, now replaced and the headquarters of Dreweatt-Neate. *Jim Irving 181* □ *(B1)*

Kimbers almshouses, Cheap Street. Two facing terraces of cottages stretched back from this entrance. They were built in 1795 and demolished during the 1950s. During the 1940s and 1950s this fine building stood empty, its window openings shored-up. New almshouses had been built in Kennet Road at the end of the 1930s. *West Berkshire Museum 1979.72.200*

40 Original gateway and gates from the Cheap Street building, transferred to the new Kimbers almshouses, Kennet Road. *Jim Irving 169*□

The western half of Kimbers almshouses. Newbury has an unusually large number of almshouses, some founded several centuries ago by local merchants. In the past they catered for widows and the 'deserving poor'. Today they provide homes for people who, for example, may not meet the local authority's criteria for housing allocation. *West Berkshire Museum 1979.72.292* 41

Kennet Road, 1953, with West Mills in the background. The tall storage building has since been converted to flats and the mill itself was destroyed by fire in 1965. The old cottages to the right have been demolished. *Jim Irving 54(C1)*

Cheap Street, late 1950s. Note the narrow pavements, despite the amount of traffic then using this road. Most buildings to the left were demolished around 1970 for the first stage of the Kennet Centre, but Fisher's greengrocery business still continues via their long-established market stall. The space next to Fisher's is where the Carlton cinema stood until 1950. To the left is Austin's bakers and confectioners shop. *Jim Irving 36*

43

Cheap Street, 1955, with St Mary's almshouses to the left. These were built in 1864 on an old foundation, but were empty at the date of this photograph and demolished 1971. The buildings beyond, to Market Street corner, still remain. *Jim Irving 189*

Newbury Cattle Market, 1953. As befitted a market town, there were two sales of livestock each week at the cattle market, which was sited where the bus station and adjacent car park is now. The town had its own abattoir off Faraday Road. *Jim Irving 51*□

Shergold's auction at their Wharf Street premises during the 1950s. Each week they held a sale of eggs, poultry, game, vegetables and other local produce and fortnightly a sale of household effects. The auction room closed in 1988 and is now The Hogshead public house. *This image is from a painting by Marjorie Heather, the renowned Newbury artist.*

After the 1943 bombing of the Council Schools, Newbury's secondary modern education was transferred to Shaw House. Boys and girls used separate sections of the building until a new boys' school was developed at Wash Common. Some boys remained at Shaw until 1954 (as this 1953 photograph shows) because Park House could not accommodate all of the pupils until its extension was completed. *Jim Irving 4*

48   P E (physical education) at Shaw House School 1955/6. *Jim Irving 110C3*

Typing class at Shaw House School 1955/6. *Jim Irving 111C2*

Schools provided lunches for the pupils and staff. The bigger schools such as Shaw House, shown here in 1955/6, had their own kitchens. *Jim Irving 114C2*

Often the main hall of a school was converted into a dining room each day, but in this unidentified school the children had to eat at their desks. *Jim Irving 117B2*

School dinners and school milk were part of the government's concern with the health of the nation. Chest diseases, especially tuberculosis, were another concern and for two decades everyone was encouraged to have their chest regularly X-rayed in mobile units which travelled around each region. This photograph was taken at Newbury Wharf in 1955.
Jim Irving 187□

Pupils were each entitled to a third of a pint of milk each day. Here, milk monitors at Park House School are carrying their allocation to their classroom in 1964. *Jim Irving 254*

Park House School extension under construction in 1954. A prefabricated system is used to speed completion. The first phase of the school, based in the former private house on the site, had opened in September 1952. There was cooperation between St Bartholomew's and Park House with pupils being exchanged for tuition in specific subjects. *Jim Irving 15*□

Metalwork class at Park House School, 1955/6. *Jim Irving 111B3*

Recorder-playing at Park House School, 1955/6. *Jim Irving 114A2*

The worst bombing of Newbury took place in February 1943, when St John's Church was severely damaged, as were adjacent almshouses and the Council Schools. Fifteen people were killed and others injured. The new St John's is seen here in 1956. It was dedicated on 13th June 1957. The temporary church used until this time can be seen in front of the new building. *Jim Irving 126*

The Congregational Church, Cromwell Place in 1954. The church had been built in 1717 and enlarged 1822, but in the 1950s was found to be unsafe. It was demolished and the foundation stone of the present church laid in June 1960.
Jim Irving 12□

Bartholomew Street and Newtown Road after a heavy shower in 1954. *Jim Irving 214□*

Bartholomew Street. E C Paine, chemist's, (the photography business came later) appears to be putting up decorations for the Coronation, despite the shop front being repainted. Note the painter's handcart: this form of transport for ladders and materials was used by many builders and other tradesmen before motor vehicles became affordable. *Jim Irving A46*

Bartholomew Street, looking north from Market Street, 1957. All the buildings on the right, except for the Bricklayers Arms, were demolished around 1970. The traffic lights outside Turner Bros. is part of Newbury's first set of traffic lights, switched on by Cllr. Jack Hole, chairman of the Highways Committee, on 25th February 1957. These controlled traffic at the junction with Market Street, a key part of the one-way traffic system for the trunk roads through the town, introduced in 1950 (see page 8). *Jim Irving 190*

61

Craven Motor & Cycle Co, Bartholomew Street, about 1960. A scooter, fashionable and affordable transport for many young people, stands outside. Next door a rotating striped sign signifying a gentlemen's hairdresser can be seen. This had developed from the traditional spirally-striped pole used in previous centuries. *West Berkshire Museum 1995.72.103*

Bartholomew Street, looking south, 1954. The shops on the right-hand side were typical of the range of small and medium sized businesses in the town: Bradshaw's (hairdressers), Joseph Atkinson (confectioner), Home & Colonial Stores (grocers), Wendy (ladies hairdresser), International Tea Company (grocers), P H Sellwood (watchmaker and jeweller), R & N Fuller (tobacconist), the Regal cinema, Heather's Stores (drapers, clothiers & house furnishers), Bendy's Stores (ironmongers, china & glass). These were followed by the offices of C G Fowlie, (surveyor and estate agent), a number of accountants and the Chamber of Commerce, the entrance to the Milk Marketing Board's premises and, finally, Newbury Building Society.
Jim Irving

Marsh Lane, looking towards Northbrook Street, with Jack of Newbury's house to the left. Marks & Spencer's car park is now on the site of the gabled cottages. The large building on the right was part of The Newbury Brewery. It later became Sunstore, but was burnt down in the 1980s. In the 1950s many families still lived in the centre of the town, passageways led to terraces and squares behind the buildings fronting the three main streets. Some of the cottages could be reasonably convenient, but many were sub-standard. Some relied on external taps or pumps for their water supply and even had to share outside toilets. Most were demolished during the second half of the 20th century, but a few still stand, converted to workshops or offices. *Jim Irving 96*

Cottages in Gilder's Square, near the Bacon Arms. Note the external tap in an iron pillar. *Jim Irving 59*

It is believed that this photograph shows the rear of the building which was formerly Newbury and Speenhamland Theatre and has been converted to cottages. The theatre stood at the head of Gilder's Square, which was entered immediately west of the Bacon Arms Hotel. *Jim Irving 183□*

A print of Newbury and Speenhamland Theatre shortly after it was built in 1802. For about thirty years it traded successfully and saw many of the leading actors of the period on its stage. Theatrical performances dwindled, its elaborate portico was removed and it had many humble uses prior to its demolition in 1976. *West Berkshire Museum*

67

Cottages in Pembroke Road (off Northbrook Street) which appear to have been converted from industrial buildings. The tenant obviously takes pride in her clean windows, whilst children play happily in the street. *Jim Irving 59*

Trafalgar Place, off Bartholomew Street, 1960. *Photograph by CC Hall. West Berkshire Museum 1995.72.41*

Crown Court, off Bartholomew Street, 1960. *Photograph by CC Hall. West Berkshire Museum 1995.72.40*

Interior of R E Moore, grocers, at Rowan Drive in the early 1950s. This was one of the six shops built by the Borough of Newbury to serve the new Shaw Estate (see page 4). Many of the goods are canned or packaged, but note the glass-topped tins of loose biscuits in front of the counter. *Brice and Gill Moore*

Horse-drawn milk float in Argyle Road, 1953. In the 1950s motorised delivery vehicles replaced horses. Most people then had milk delivered to their doorstep each day. Bread, too, was delivered in this way and greengrocers with vegetables and fruit might call weekly. Grocers, butchers and coal merchants would also deliver orders made at their shops. Coal was used in most homes for fires to heat living rooms, also to provide hot water. A few people still used cooking ranges, though by the 1950s most homes in towns would have gas or electric cookers. *Jim Irving A19*

Older houses often had twisting or narrow staircases that presented a problem when moving house. This accommodation, next to The Star in London Road, has had window sashes temporarily removed to take out the larger pieces of furniture. Arthur Mitchell's shop, below, continues to sell its greengrocery, including tomatoes at 1/2d (7p) a pound and bananas at 1/6d (7.5p). *Jim Irving 191*

London Road in 1957, looking westwards. The signs of the Star Inn and Springs café can be seen, the latter converted from a house of 1700 with a fine staircase. All that survives today is St Mary's House, at the far right. *Jim Irving 59*

The thriving commercial development of Hambridge Road makes it easy to forget that much of the area was dug for gravel, leaving flooded pits, subsequently filled in and built on. Hills Ltd were major operators, as their fleet of lorries beside the gravel washing, grading and loading plant in this 1960 photograph shows. *Jim Irving 112*

The Mayor's Drive – Councillor and Mrs J H Hole are hosts. All townspeople aged 70 or over were invited to take part. Volunteer drivers were asked to collect named guests, take them for a one-hour drive and meet at Greenham Common at 4 pm for tea. Tea was eaten in the cars so that those who couldn't easily get out of a vehicle could take part. Teas in individual boxes were prepared beforehand and on arrival at Greenham, drivers were asked to collect the boxes and cups of tea for their passengers. In July 1950, 374 old people arrived at Greenham in 94 cars and three coaches. *West Berkshire Museum 1995.11.7*

Newbury Wharf when it was Newbury's bus station. The Granary housed bus company offices, newsagents and a café. On the right of the photograph is the Corner House Café, the rest of Kendrick House was occupied by a doctors' surgery.
West Berkshire Museum 1992.29

Newbury railway station, 1958. Snow shows clearly the pattern of the through lines and those leading from the main platforms and bays. The Lambourn Valley train used the bay to the side of the 'up' platform, on the left. A goods and livestock platform is at the right, although the main goods yard was at the far side of the station, where Sainsbury's and Scats are now built. *Jim Irving 60*

A group of young people involved in a competition to win six Vespa scooters, staged in connection with *Film Review* and Toblerone, at the Forum cinema. During the late 1950s and 1960s the cinema had a go-ahead manager, Noel Briggs, who brought much publicity to the cinema through competitions and events that he organised, usually connected with the films being shown. *West Berkshire Museum 1998.80.106*

Window display for a Festival of Britain competition at Brice Gould & Co, 114, Bartholomew Street. This grocer's shop specialised in coffee and many will recall the rich aroma from the roaster in the shop. *Photograph by H Torpey.*
Brice and Gill Moore

Toomer's float for the Festival of Britain carnival procession. This contrasted contemporary household goods which they sold, with an impression of what might have been available at their founding in 1692. *West Berkshire Museum 2001.41*

Black Beetle Jazz Band, one of the six jazz bands in the Festival of Britain procession. Formed at AERE Harwell, it was augmented for this occasion. The procession is lining up in Enborne Road and the lorry is one loaned following the Borough Council's plea to owners of lorries or trailers to make them available for the carnival procession. *Graham Curtis*

Coronation Street Party, Stroud Green, 1953. Greenham Road passes in the background. Many street parties were organised in the town and duly reported in the *Newbury Weekly News*. *Photograph by Ian Baines. Mrs Joan Gibbs*

Coronation Street party, Russell Road. The tea party for 58 children was arranged around separate tables. The lady with the large teapot is Mrs Parton who, with Mrs Dyson, had organised four street parties prior to this one. Several of the adult helpers had attended the first party (1935) as children. *Mrs Chris Evans*

Fancy Dress competition, Russell Road. Following the party, children were taken to Northcroft for sports and returned to Russell Road for the fancy dress competition depicted here. Mrs Dyson can be seen near the left of the picture, Mrs Parton third from the right at the back. The older inhabitants of the street were not forgotten and dancing in the street continued until midnight! *Mrs Chris Evans*

86   E P Timmins, fruiterer's, 130/131, Bartholomew Street, window display for the Coronation window-dressing competition.
West Museum D3161.2

Even manufacturers joined in the Coronation celebrations. Here Hovis has decorated its Town Mill building.
West Berkshire Museum 1983.29.41

Hovis's float for the Coronation carnival procession, depicting tea in an English cottage garden. Note the 'television aerial' beginning to become a familiar sight at that time. *Photograph by M & H Studios. West Berkshire Museum 1983.29.23*

Coronation carnival float of Brice Gould & Co, with Mr R E Moore, the proprietor, roasting coffee. His sons, daughter in law and an assistant are dressed for the parts of producers and consumers. Also of interest is the poster advertising that the eminent musicians, William Pleeth and Julian Bream, were to play at the Corn Exchange with Gerald Finzi's Newbury String Players. *Brice and Gill Moore*

Toomer's float for the Coronation procession. The shops of Boots, Timothy Whites and Camp Hopson can be seen, together with a glimpse of the large crowds which gathered to watch the procession. *West Berkshire Museum 2001.37*

This photograph of Newbury library in 1955 shows the system operating then to record books loaned to users. Members had an allocation of tickets, one of which was placed in a small card 'pocket', bearing a reference to its title, removable from each book borrowed. These were then filed in narrow drawers under the date the loan expired. Cumbersome compared with today's computerised methods, it kept an efficient record of loans, but did not allow the sophisticated collation of statistics of modern systems. *Jim Irving 82*

Jim Irving, the photographer of many of the pictures in this book, supplementing his teacher's salary by working for the Post Office at Christmas 1956. Today, when many senior pupils have cars, it seems surprising to recall that in the 1950s virtually no staff apart from the head teacher would own vehicles. Staff and pupils would travel to school by cycle, bus or on foot. *Jim Irving 123*

Percy Sellwood, Honorary Archivist to the Borough of Newbury, in 1958. It is through his efforts that many records and photographs of Newbury survive. Photographs and maps were transferred to the museum in 1979 when the rest of the records were deposited for safe-keeping at the Berkshire Record Office. *Jim Irving 305*

Acknowledgements

I would like to thank the many people who have helped with the production of this book: firstly, Nicholas Battle of Countryside Books, who proposed it, and subsequently for his patience and understanding when the time-scale for its completion extended. Thanks also to Paula Leigh, editor, for her patience, assistance and skill. My wife, Kath, must also be thanked for her support, particularly when summer pleasures and my domestic tasks were put aside whilst the book was prepared.

The staff of Newbury Reference Library were most helpful on the many occasions when I referred to the microfilm copies of the *Newbury Weekly News* held by them. I thank also Julian May, Deputy News Editor, for assisting my failed attempt to reproduce photographs from 1950s' copies of the paper. The paper does, of course, provide an excellent contemporary record of the events of the decade, which I used extensively. Resulting from a letter published in the *Newbury Weekly News*, several private owners of photographs of the Festival of Britain and Coronation celebrations came forward. Each is acknowledged alongside the reproductions of their photographs, but I would like to express my real gratitude to them, both for making their pictures available and trusting me with the originals, not all of which it was possible to use.

The majority of the photographs have come from two sources. West Berkshire Museum has around three thousand images of the area, which are safely kept for reference by this and future generations. I am grateful to the museum for allowing use of some of their images and thank Amanda Loaring, head of the service, and especially Jane Burrell, who spent much time retrieving photographs from their storage and producing electronic copies. However, the book would not have been achievable without Jim Irving. He has produced an amazing collection of images of Newbury since coming to the town around 1950. He has held all major offices with Newbury Camera Club in the ensuing half century and his skill has been acknowledged nationally by his election as a Fellow of the Royal Photographic Society. In addition he could not have been more helpful to me in readily making available his photographs during several visits to his home and producing prints to be copied for this publication and for that I cannot thank him enough.

Tony Higgott

Index